Praise for Twenty Three Cats from Chinese Teachers

"*Twenty Three Cats* is a very cute story, an easy read for beginning Chinese learners. Repetitions in the vocabulary and sentence structure help novice students learn easily. The drawings are vivid and thoughtful to reflect the reading. I love that the pinyin is provided on the opposite page for a quick reference, and not next to the characters directly. I also find it useful for novice learners to have an English version of the story as well as a glossary towards the end of the book." - *Treena Larson, Chinese and DE&I Teacher, University of Chicago Laboratory Schools*

"*Twenty Three Cats* is fun and gives students the earliest possible sense of achievement. Comprehensible Input is where it's at. Kudos to Jeff for producing an excellent first book for any beginner class. We will be using it in our online classes!" – *Robin Rynhart, President, ChineseHomework.ie*

"What a whimsical story about a boy and his lovely cats! The repetition is wonderful for reading aloud. Young readers will feel so successful to finish reading a book! The illustrations can be used to further extend the discussion in target language. I found myself reading this story with a smile. You should definitely check it out!" – *Sara Chao, High School Chinese Teacher, New Trier Township High School; board member, Chinese Language Association of Secondary-Elementary Schools*

"I'm really excited about this book. Throughout 5,000 years of Chinese history, books like San Zi Jing (Three Character Classic) have played a very important role in children's early learning. Twenty Three Cats follows this tradition. It is written using only 101 different Chinese words, all of which (except for one) are in HSK1 level. I hope it will help English speaking people to start learning about Chinese language and culture. – *Jiahui Zhang, Principal, Pittsburgh Chinese School*

"**This is a simple but creative and helpful book** for beginning Chinese language learners!" – *Shijuan Liu, Associate Professor of Chinese, Indiana University of Pennsylvania*

"**This is a very good book for beginners to learn Chinese** and master the HSK1 vocabulary. This book can not only attract children's attention, but is also a very good resource for adult learners. I think this book is a perfect option for children and adult learners who are looking for a way to learn basic Chinese." – *Tong Chen, Lecturer in Chinese, Massachusetts Institute of Technology Global Languages; board member, Chinese Teachers Association*

"**This is a lovely story full of imagination.** The dialogues make it easy for beginner readers to understand, and the repetition of high-frequency words deepens the memory of language. Kids will be interested in learning Chinese and then actually learn it." - *Rongrong Lin, Chinese Teacher, New Trier High School, Northfield IL*

"**This is an engaging and fun story for beginners** in learning Chinese, with lots of high-frequency words and expressions repeated throughout. While building up learners' confidence and interest, this book is also an excellent resource for Chinese teachers with a variety of uses. Thank you for making another great book in Chinese for us!" - *Jin Yin, Chinese Language Teacher, University of Chicago Lab Schools*

"***Twenty Three Cats* will be a good friend to Chinese beginners.** As a Chinese language teacher, I know that combining new words into stories is a very effective teaching method. Interesting plots and pictures can help students form schema memory and enhance those memories, making Chinese learning more attractive." - *Yang Jiali, Chinese Language Teacher, Confucius Institute in Sofia, Bulgaria*

Twenty Three Cats

二十三隻貓

An Easy-to-Read Story in Traditional Chinese and Pinyin,

101 Word Vocabulary

Written by Jeff Pepper

Illustrated by Pui Jo Ng

Published in the United States by Imagin8 Press LLC, Verona, Pennsylvania, US. For information, contact us at info@imagin8press.com, or visit www.imagin8press.com.

Our books may be purchased directly in quantity at a reduced price, contact us for details.

Imagin8 Press, the Imagin8 logo and the sail image are all trademarks of Imagin8 Press LLC.

Written and designed by Jeff Pepper
Illustrations by Pui Jo Ng
Audiobook narration by Junyou Chen

Many thanks to Xiao Hui Wang, Tong Chen, Shijuan Liu, Jiali Yang, Sara Chao, Maurice Leung and Arnaud Ysmal for their help in reviewing the manuscript, and thanks to our incredibly talented artist Pui Jo Ng for the illustrations.

ISBN: 978-1952601354
Version 10

You can listen to this book for free. A complete Chinese language audiobook is on YouTube. Search for the Imagin8 Press channel, where you will find the audiobook for this and all of our other fiction books.

Our website, www.imagin8press.com, provides a direct link to the YouTube audiobook, a link that you can use to download the audiobook to your computer, and information about all of our books.

Introduction

Last summer a customer contacted us at Imagin8 Press to ask if we had any books written using the HSK1 vocabulary, which is the first 150 words taught to beginning students of the Chinese language. Most of our fiction books are written using the 600 words of HSK3, and a few use 1200 words or even more. I wrote back and said that, sadly, there was no way anyone could possibly tell a story using such a minimal vocabulary. But as the weeks went by, I just couldn't shake the feeling that somewhere, somehow, there must be a story lurking in that tiny set of Chinese words.

Then I remembered the wonderful children's books written by Dr. Seuss. His first and most famous, *The Cat in the Hat*, used just 236 different English words. So I decided to give it a try, and this book is the result. It uses just 100 of the 150 words in HSK1. I also had to add one more word, 隻 (zhī), a measure word for animals, because there's just no way to talk about dogs and cats in Chinese without using 隻.

As for the number of cats in the story... well, you probably know the Dr. Seuss short story called *Too Many Daves*, about a nice lady named Mrs. McCave who had twenty three sons and she named them all Dave.

So, here's to you, Dr. Seuss. There are no Daves here, but we do have twenty three cats.

Enjoy the book!

Jeff Pepper
Pittsburgh, Pennsylvania, USA
February, 2021
Revised June, 2025

Wǒ jiā yǒu èr shí sān zhī māo.

Wǒ de jiā hěn xiǎo.

Zhè shì yígè hěn hǎo de xiǎo jiā.

我家有二十三隻貓。

我的家很小。

這是一個很好的小家。

Wǒ shì yígè xuéshēng.

Wǒ yígè rén zhù zài Zhōngguó Běijīng.

Wǒ de māma hé bàba bú zhù zài Běijīng.

我是一個學生。

我一個人住在中國北京。

我的媽媽和爸爸不住在北京。

Wǒ xǐhuān wǒ de yǐzi hé zhuōzi.

Wǔ zhī māo zuò zài wǒ de yǐzi shàng.

Bā zhī māo zuò zài wǒ de zhuōzi xià.

我喜歡我的椅子和桌子。

五隻貓坐在我的椅子上。

八隻貓坐在我的桌子下。

Wǒ ài wǒ de shū.

Liù zhī māo zuò zài wǒ de shū shàng.

Wǒ bùnéng dú wǒ de shū.

我愛我的書。

六隻貓坐在我的書上。

我不能讀我的書。

Wǒ yǒu yígè diànnǎo.

Wǒ zài diànnǎo shàng kàn diànshì.

Sān zhī māo zuò zài wǒ de diànnǎo shàng.

我有一個電腦。

我在電腦上看電視。

三隻貓坐在我的電腦上。

Nàxiē māo bùnéng kàn diànshì.

Shí bā zhī māo zài kàn diànshì.

Tāmen xiàwǔ dōu zài kàn diànyǐng.

那些貓不能看電視。

二十隻貓在看電視。

他們下午都在看電影。

Wǒ jiā de hòumiàn shì yígè Zhōngguó fàndiàn.

Māo xǐhuān qù fàndiàn.

Māo chī Zhōngguó cài, hē Zhōngguó chá.

我家的後面是一個中國飯店。

貓喜歡去飯店。

貓吃中國菜，喝中國茶。

Zuótiān shàngwǔ wǒ de péngyǒu lái wǒ jiā.

Tā shì wǒ xuéxiào de tóngxué.

Tā kànjiàn le hěnduō māo.

昨天上午我的朋友來我家。

她是我學校的同學。

她看見了很多貓。

Tā shuō, "Nǐ jiā yǒu duōshǎo zhī māo?"

Wǒ shuō, "Èr shí sān zhī māo."

Tā shuō, "Wǒ néng zuò zài nǎlǐ?"

她說，"你家有多少隻貓？"

我說，"二十三隻貓。"

她說，"我能坐在哪裡？"

Wǒmen xiǎng zuò xià lái hē bēi chá.

Wǒmen bù néng zuò. Yǐzi shàng yǒu māo.

Wǒ shuō, "Duìbùqǐ, jīntiān méiyǒu chá."

我們想坐下來喝杯茶。

我們不能坐。椅子上有貓。

我說，“對不起，今天沒有茶。”

Wǒmen xiǎng chī Zhōngguó cài.

Wǒmen bù néng chī Zhōngguó cài. Māo chīle nà ge
Zhōngguó cài.

Wǒ shuō, "Duìbùqǐ, jīntiān méiyǒu Zhōngguó cài."

我們想吃中國菜。

我們不能吃中國菜。貓吃了那個中國菜。

我說，“對不起，今天沒有中國菜。”

Wǒmen xiǎng kàn shū, yě xiǎng xuéxí.

Wǒmen bù néng xuéxí. Māo zuò zài wǒ de shū shàng.

Wǒ shuō, "Duìbùqǐ, jīntiān bù xuéxí le."

我們想看書，也想學習。

我們不能學習。貓坐在我的書上。

我說，“對不起，今天不學習了。”

Wǒ de péngyǒu shuō, "Nǐ de māo tài duō le!"

Wǒ shuō, "Wǒ zěnme zuò?"

Wǒ de péngyǒu shuō, "Tīng wǒ shuō!"

我的朋友說，"你的貓太多了！"

我說，"我怎麼做？"

我的朋友說，"聽我說！"

“Qǐng mǎi yì zhī gǒu. Gǒu xǐhuān chī māo.”

Wǒ shuō, “Xièxie. Wǒ huì mǎi yì zhī gǒu.”

Wǒ de péngyǒu huí le tāde jiā.

"請買一隻狗。狗喜歡吃貓。"

我說，"謝謝。我會買一隻狗。"

我的朋友回了她的家。

Jīntiān wǒ qù le shāngdiàn.

Wǒ shuō, "Xiānsheng, nǐ yǒu gǒu ma?"

Nàge rén shuō, "Yǒu, wǒmen yǒu hěnduō zhī gǒu."

今天我去了商店。

我說，“先生，你有狗嗎？”

那個人說，“有，我們有很多隻狗。”

Nàge rén shuō, "Nǐ xiǎng mǎi yì zhī gǒu ma?"

Wǒ shuō, "Xiǎng, wǒ xiǎng mǎi yì zhī dà gǒu."

Wǒ shuō, "Wǒ tīng shuō gǒu chī māo."

那個人說，"你想買一隻狗嗎？"

我說，"想，我想買一隻大狗。"

我說，"我聽說狗吃貓。"

Nàge rén shuō, "Zhè shì yì zhī hǎo gǒu."

Wǒ mǎi le nà zhī gǒu. Nàge rén shuō, "Xièxie."

Wǒ shuō, "Búkèqì. Zàijiàn."

那個人說，"這是一隻好狗。"

我買了那隻狗。那個人說，"謝謝。"

我說，"不客氣。再見。"

Gǒu hé wǒ huí le wǒ jiā.

Gǒu kànjiàn le māo.

Gǒu xiǎng, "Zhèlǐ de māo tài duō le."

狗和我回了我家。

狗看見了貓。

狗想，"這裡的貓太多了。"

Yì zhī māo shuō, "Nà shì yì zhī dà gǒu."

Yì zhī māo shuō, "Nà zhī gǒu xiǎng chī diǎn dōngxi."

Yì zhī māo shuō, "Wǒmen yǒu shuǐguǒ!"

一隻貓說，"那是一隻大狗。"

一隻貓說，"那隻狗想吃點東西。"

一隻貓說，"我們有水果！"

Yì zhī māo shuō, "Wǒ de péngyǒu, nǐ xiǎng chī yì diǎn'er shuǐguǒ ma?"

Gǒu shuō, "Shì de, xièxie."

Gǒu chī le yì diǎn'er shuǐguǒ.

一隻貓說，"我的朋友，你想吃一點兒水果嗎？"

狗說，"是的，謝謝。"

狗吃了一點兒水果。

Māo shuō, "Nǐ xǐhuān shuǐguǒ ma?"

Gǒu shuō, "Shì de, wǒ xǐhuān zhège shuǐguǒ!"

Māo shuō, "Wǒmen yǒu hěnduō shuǐguǒ."

貓說，"你喜歡水果嗎？"

狗說，"是的，我喜歡這個水果！"

貓說，"我們有很多水果。"

Māo shuō, "Wǒ de péngyǒu, nǐ xiǎng chī shí kuài shuǐguǒ ma?"

Gǒu shuō, "Xiǎng, xièxie."

Nà zhī gǒu chīle shí kuài shuǐguǒ.

貓說，"我的朋友，你想吃十塊水果嗎？"

狗說，"想，謝謝。"

那隻狗吃了十塊水果。

Gǒu hěn gāoxìng.

Èr shí sān zhī māo hěn gāoxìng.

Gǒu qù shuìjiào le.

狗很高興。

二十三隻貓很高興。

狗去睡覺了。

Xiànzài, gǒu hé māo shì hǎo péngyǒu le.

Wǒ shuō, "Nǐ huì chī zhè xiē māo ma?"

Gǒu shuō, "Shénme?"

現在，狗和貓是好朋友了。

我說，"你會吃這些貓嗎？"

狗說，"什麼？"

Gǒu shuō, "Duìbùqǐ, zhè xiē māo shì wǒ de péngyǒu."

Gǒu shuō, "Wǒ bù xiǎng chī wǒ de péngyǒu."

Wǒ shuō, "Méiguānxì, nǐ shì hǎo gǒu, zhèxiē māo shì hǎo māo."

狗說，"對不起，這些貓是我的朋友。"

狗說，"我不想吃我的朋友。"

我說，"沒關係，你是好狗，這些貓是好貓。"

Xiànzài wǒ hé èr shí sān zhī māo hé yì zhī gǒu zhù zài wǒjiā.

Wǒmen xiàwǔ kàn diànyǐng.

Wǒmen dōu hěn gāoxìng.

現在我和二十三隻貓和一隻狗住在我家。

我們下午看電影。

我們都很高興。

Twenty Three Cats

In my house are twenty three cats.
My house is very small.
It is a good little house.

I am a student.
I live alone in Beijing China.
My parents don't live in Beijing.

I like my chair and table.
Five cats sit on my chair.
Eight cats sit under my table.

I love my books.
Six cats sit on my books.
I cannot read my books.

I have a computer.
I watch television on my computer.
Three cats sit on top of my computer.

Those cats cannot watch television.
Twenty cats watch television.
They watch movies all afternoon.

Behind my house is a Chinese restaurant.

The cats like to go to the restaurant.

The cats eat Chinese food and drink Chinese tea.

Yesterday morning my friend came to my house.

She is my classmate in school.

She saw a lot of cats.

She said, "How many cats live in your house?"

I said, "Twenty three cats."

She said, "Where can I sit down? "

We wanted to sit and drink a cup of tea.

We could not sit. There were cats on the chairs.

I said, "Sorry, no tea today."

We wanted to eat Chinese food.

We could not eat Chinese food. The cats ate all the Chinese food.

I said, "Sorry, no Chinese food today."

We wanted to read books and study.

We could not study. The cats were sitting on my books.

I said, "Sorry, no studying today."

My friend said, "You have too many cats!"

I said, "What should I do?"

My friend said, "Listen to me!"

"Please buy a dog. Dogs like to eat cats."
I said, "Thank you. I will buy a dog."
My friend went back to her house.

Today I went to the store.
I said, "Sir, do you have dogs?"
The man said, "Yes, we have many dogs."

The man said, "Do you want to buy a dog?"
I said, "Yes, I want to buy a big dog."
I said, "I heard that dogs eat cats."

The man said, "here is a good dog."
I bought the dog. The man said, "Thank you."
I said, "You're welcome. Goodbye."

The dog and I returned to my house.
The dog saw the cats.
The dog thought, "There are too many cats here."

One cat said, "That's a big dog."
One cat said, "That dog wants to eat something."
One cat said, "We have some fruit!"

One cat said, "My friend, do you want a piece of fruit?"
The dog said, "Yes, thank you."
The dog ate the piece of fruit.

The cat said, "Do you like the fruit?"

The dog said, "Yes, I like this fruit!"

The cat said, "We have a lot of fruit."

The cat said, "My friend, do you want ten pieces of fruit?"

The dog said, "Yes, thank you."

The dog ate the ten pieces of fruit.

The dog was very happy.

The twenty three cats were happy.

The dog went to sleep.

Now the dog and the cats are good friends.

I said, "Will you eat these cats?"

The dog said, "What?"

The dog said, "Sorry, these cats are my friends."

The dog said, "I do not want to eat my friends."

I said, "It doesn't matter. These are good cats. And you are a good dog."

Now I live with twenty three cats and one dog.

We watch movies in the afternoon.

We are all very happy.

Glossary

These is a complete list of all 150 Chinese words in the HSK1 vocabulary. Of those, 100 of them are used in this book, and those are indicated with a "✓" in the last column.

There's also one measure word, 隻 (zhī), that is used in the book but is not included in HSK1. It's indicated with a "NEW" in the last column.

Chinese	Pinyin	English	Used?
愛	ài	to love	✓
八	bā	eight	✓
爸爸	bàba	father	✓
北京	Běijīng	Beijing	✓
杯子	bēizi	cup	✓
本	běn	<measure word>	
不	bù	no, not	✓
不客氣	búkèqì	you're welcome	✓
菜	cài	food, dish	✓
茶	chá	tea	✓
吃	chī	to eat	✓
出租車	chūzūchē	taxi	
大	dà	big	✓
打電話	dǎdiànhuà	to call on phone	
的	de	of	✓
點	diǎn	<measure word>	✓

电脑	diànnǎo	computer	✓
电视	diànshì	television	✓
电影	diànyǐng	movie	✓
東西	dōngxi	thing	✓
都	dōu	all	✓
讀	dú	to read	✓
對不起	duìbùqǐ	sorry	✓
多	duō	many, much	✓
多少	duōshǎo	how many, how much	✓
二	èr	two	✓
兒子	érzi	son	
飯店	fàndiàn	restaurant	✓
飛機	fēijī	airplane	
分鐘	fēnzhōng	minute	
高興	gāoxìng	happy	✓
個	gè	one, a, an	✓
工作	gōngzuò	work	
狗	gǒu	dog	✓
漢語	hànyǔ	mandarin Chinese	
好	hǎo	good	✓
和	hé	and	✓
喝	hē	to drink	✓
很	hěn	quite, very	✓
後面	hòumiàn	behind	✓

回	huí	to return	✔
會	huì	can	✔
火車站	huǒchēzhàn	train station	
幾	jǐ	a few, how many	
家	jiā	home	✔
叫	jiào	to call	
今天	jīntiān	today	✔
九	jiǔ	nine	
開	kāi	open	
看	kàn	to look	✔
看見	kànjiàn	to see	✔
塊	kuài	<measure word>	✔
來	lái	to come	✔
老師	lǎoshī	teacher	
了	le	<indicates completion>	✔
冷	lěng	cold	
裡面	lǐmiàn	inside	
零	líng	zero	
六	liù	six	✔
嗎	ma	<indicates question>	✔
買	mǎi	to buy	✔
媽媽	māma	mother	✔
貓	māo	cat	✔
沒	méi	no	✔
沒關係	méiguānxì	it doesn't matter	✔

米飯	mǐfàn	rice	
明天	míngtiān	tomorrow	
名字	míngzì	name	
那(兒), 那裡	nà(er), nàlǐ	that, there	✓
哪(儿), 哪里	nǎ(er), nǎlǐ	which?, where?	✓
呢	ne	<particle>	
能	néng	to be able to	✓
你	nǐ	you	✓
年	nián	year	
你們	nǐmen	you (plural)	
女兒	nǚér	daughter	
朋友	péngyǒu	friend	✓
漂亮	piàoliàng	beautiful	
蘋果	píngguǒ	apple	
七	qī	seven	
錢	qián	money	
前面	qiánmiàn	front	
請	qǐng	please	✓
去	qù	to go	✓
熱	rè	hot	
人	rén	person	✓
認識	rènshi	to know	
日	rì	day	
三	sān	three	✓

上	shàng	up, above	✓
商店	shāngdiàn	store	✓
上午	shàngwǔ	morning	✓
少	shǎo	few, little	✓
什麼	shénme	what, why	✓
十	shí	ten	✓
是	shì	to be	✓
時候	shíhou	time	
書	shū	book	✓
誰	shuí	who	
水	shuǐ	water	
水果	shuǐguǒ	fruit	✓
睡覺	shuìjiào	to sleep	✓
說(話)	shuō(huà)	to speak	✓
四	sì	four	
歲	suì	year	
他	tā	he, him	
她	tā	she, her	✓
太	tài	too much	✓
他們	tāmen	they	✓
她們	tāmen	they (females)	
天氣	tiānqì	weather	
聽	tīng	to listen	✓
同學	tóngxué	schoolmate	✓
餵	wèi	hello	

我	wǒ	I, me	✓
我們	wǒmen	we, us	✓
五	wǔ	five	✓
下	xià	under, down	✓
想	xiǎng	to want, to think	✓
先生	xiānsheng	Mister, sir	✓
現在	xiànzài	now	✓
小	xiǎo	small	✓
小姐	xiǎojiě	Miss	
下午	xiàwǔ	afternoon	✓
下雨	xiàyǔ	rain	
寫	xiě	to write	
些	xiē	some	✓
謝謝	xièxie	thank you	✓
喜歡	xǐhuān	to like	✓
星期	xīngqī	week	
學生	xuéshēng	student	✓
學習	xuéxí	to study	✓
學校	xuéxiào	school	✓
一	yī	one	✓
衣服	yīfu	clothing	
醫生	yīshēng	doctor	
醫院	yīyuàn	hospital	
椅子	yǐzi	chair	✓

有	yǒu	to have	✓
月	yuè	month	
在	zài	in, at	✓
再見	zàijiàn	goodbye	✓
怎麼	zěnme	how	✓
怎麼樣	zěnmeyàng	how about	
這(兒), 這裡	zhè(r), zhèlǐ	this, here	✓
隻	zhī	<measure word>	NEW
中國	Zhōngguó	China	✓
中午	zhōngwǔ	noon	
住	zhù	to live	✓
桌子	zhuōzi	desk	✓
字	zì	Chinese character	
做	zuò	to do	✓
坐	zuò	to sit	✓
昨天	zuótiān	yesterday	✓

About the Author

Jeff Pepper is President and CEO of Imagin8 Press, and has written dozens of books about Chinese language and culture. Over his thirty-five year career he has founded and led several successful computer software firms, including one that became a publicly traded company. He's authored two software related books and was awarded three U.S. software patents.